MW00830942

MEDITATIONS
on God's Character

TIFFANY DICKERSON

HOW TO USE
THIS RESOURCE

Biblical meditation is a discipline of thinking about and considering the truths of God's Word. This practice looks like spending extended time reflecting on what God is communicating through His Word and what it teaches us about Him. Spending time reading and studying God's Word is of utmost importance, and we plant those truths in our hearts when we spend time pondering what they truly mean for us and for our lives. We can practice meditation through prayer, journaling, memorizing Scripture, or simply dwelling on biblical truths throughout the day.

Psalm 119:14–16 says, "I rejoice in the way revealed by your decrees as much as in all riches. I will meditate on your precepts and think about your ways. I will delight in your statutes; I will not forget your word."

Biblical meditation serves as a discipline that allows us to carefully consider and weigh the truths of Scripture so that they lay fresh in our hearts. When we meditate on God's Word, it is easier to call it to mind when we need God's wisdom and instruction.

Biblical meditation can happen all day long. Psalm 1:2 says, "his delight is in the Lord's instruction, and he meditates on it day and night." We can practice biblical meditation anytime and anywhere. We can practice it while going on a walk, while folding laundry, while doing the dishes, while getting ready for bed, and every moment in between.

As you open this booklet, our hope is that it will guide you through the practice of biblical meditation for 31 days. This resource will provide Scripture to read throughout the day, prompts to encourage a thoughtful understanding of God's Word, and prayer time to ask for God's help. We hope you will find a greater delight in God's Word, a deeper knowledge and understanding of who God is, and feel better equipped to practice biblical meditation on your own.

Tips for Daily Reading

- Set a daily alarm clock on your phone for each reading time: morning, midday, and evening.

- Leave this booklet lying around common areas so that you will be reminded to use it.

- Leave this booklet on your kitchen table or countertop to use during meal times.

- Place this booklet near your Bible to use as a companion resource in your reading times.

- Ask a friend to use this resource alongside you for accountability.

- Use a journal alongside this resource as a place for you to include longer thoughts and prayers.

INTRODUCTION

God's character is a mystery many humans have tried to articulate since the moment Moses recorded God saying, "Let there be..." (Genesis 1). But even though some elements of His character remain a mystery, God has revealed many aspects of His character in the Bible. From Genesis to Revelation, God's character is on display through His sovereignty, faithfulness, goodness, holiness, and truth, to name just a few. Yet God does not have to reveal His entire character in order for us to know, love, and trust Him. Second Peter 1:3 tells us, "His divine power has given us everything required for life and godliness through the knowledge of him who called us by his own glory and goodness." This means that God has given us everything we need to know about Him through His Word, Jesus Christ, and the Holy Spirit.

Over the next 31 days, daily Scripture passages and short reflection exercises will teach us about God's many character traits. Each day, as you learn more about who God is and how He works, allow yourself to live in awe and thankfulness for our great God. Cultivate a heart that yearns to know all that God reveals about Himself across the pages of Scripture. By no means is this list exhaustive. You may also notice that several attributes of God's character repeat; this includes *righteous*, *faithful*, *holy*, *loving*, *truth*, *unchanging*, and *shepherd*. As you meditate on these attributes multiple times, it is our prayer that your understanding of these attributes will deepen and grow.

We also pray that this booklet would provide you a glimpse into God's infinite character, for that glimpse gives us all we need as we await Jesus's return and the eternal gift of dwelling with God forever. Until that day comes, let us intentionally pursue God's character so that we can become more like Him and point others to Him.

FROM GENESIS TO
REVELATION,

God's character

IS ON DISPLAY.

CONTENTS

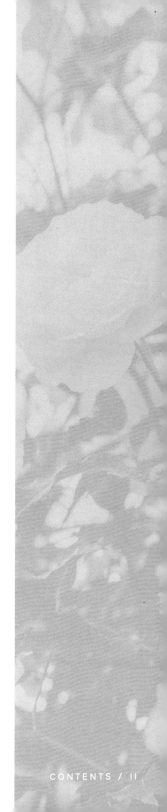

DAY 01: CREATOR

In the beginning God created the heavens and the earth.

GENESIS 1:1

*Read each verse entry below, and focus on the words in **bold** each time. Journal your thoughts and observations in response to the **bolded** words. What does this teach you about God and His character as our Creator?*

In the beginning God created the heavens and the earth.

In the beginning God created the heavens and the earth.

In the beginning **God created** the heavens and the earth.

In the beginning God created **the heavens and the earth**.

JOURNAL

MIDDAY

Read Genesis 1:1 again.

PRAY

Take some time to ponder the intricacies of God's creation. Consider the complexities of the human body, the beauty of nature, and the vast species of animals. Thank the Lord for His creativity and the gift of life and beauty in this world. Give Him praise for the masterpiece of your life and the universe He made for His glory.

Read Genesis 1:1 one last time.

As you end your day, think about that very first day when there was evening and morning. God gave us twenty-four hours each day to see the goodness of His creation. Write a list of all the things in His creation you experienced today and how they point to God as the perfect Creator.

RESPOND

DAY 02: I AM

God replied to Moses, "I AM WHO I AM. This is what you are to say to the Israelites: I AM has sent me to you." God also said to Moses, "Say this to the Israelites: The Lord, the God of your ancestors, the God of Abraham, the God of Isaac, and the God of Jacob, has sent me to you. This is my name forever; this is how I am to be remembered in every generation.

EXODUS 3:14–15

Read Exodus 3:14–15

RESPOND

In Exodus 3, God reveals His character to Moses.
With the name "I AM," God tells Moses everything
he needs to know about God's character: God is who
He says He is, and He is faithful to His Word and all
His promises. God had not forgotten about His people
enslaved in Egypt. He had not forgotten His promises
to Abraham, Isaac, and Jacob. He is "I AM" from
generation to generation. Take a few moments to
write down how God has been "I AM" in your life.
How has He been faithful?

Read Exodus 3:14–15 again.

RESPOND

What other character traits of God does the name "I AM" bring to mind?

RESPOND

How has God proven His faithfulness "in every generation"?

RESPOND

In what ways are you comforted by "I AM" and His faithfulness to all generations?

RESPOND

How do you see the name "I AM" fulfilled in Christ? How has Jesus kept God's promise of faithfulness from generation to generation?

Read Exodus 3:14–15 one more time.

Take a few moments to write a prayer, thanking God for His faithfulness to all generations through Jesus. Ask Him to remind you each day that He is "I AM." He is in complete control, and you can call on Him in the good times, the difficult times, the sad times, and the glad times.

PRAY

DAY 03: POWERFUL

Do you not know? Have you not heard? The Lord is the everlasting God, the Creator of the whole earth. He never becomes faint or weary; there is no limit to his understanding. He gives strength to the faint and strengthens the powerless. Youths may become faint and weary, and young men stumble and fall, but those who trust in the Lord will renew their strength; they will soar on wings like eagles; they will run and not become weary, they will walk and not faint.

ISAIAH 40:28–31

Read Isaiah 40:28–31 aloud.

RESPOND

What do these verses reveal about God's character?
Write a list of all the character traits of God you see
in these verses.

MEDITATE

Choose one of these characteristics to meditate on
this morning as you go to work, watch your children,
or even run errands.

MIDDAY

Read Isaiah 40:28–31 again.

RESPOND

How is God different from man in these verses? Write a list to compare and contrast what God can do and what man cannot do.

RESPOND

God is powerful and has control over every aspect of His creation and our lives. What worry or weakness do you need to give to His capable hands?

PRAY

Do you believe God is all-powerful? Do you believe He can help you in your current circumstances? If yes, pray in boldness for His help. If not, pray for Him to grow your faith in His power over everything.

Read Isaiah 40:28–31 one more time.

VISUALIZE

Visualize handing God your greatest weakness, worry, and fear. Now, picture Him renewing your strength as you soar on wings like an eagle in freedom from weakness, as you run from your worry without allowing it to weary you, and as you walk away from your fear without growing faint or looking back.

PRAY

Write a prayer of thanksgiving to God for His power over all creation and His strength to help you overcome difficult things in your life.

DAY 04: RIGHTEOUS

"Look, the days are coming"—this is the Lord's declaration—"when I will raise up a Righteous Branch for David. He will reign wisely as king and administer justice and righteousness in the land. In his days Judah will be saved, and Israel will dwell securely. This is the name he will be called: The Lord Is Our Righteousness.

JEREMIAH 23:5–6

Read Jeremiah 23:5–6.

RESPOND

What word is repeated three times?
Who is this passage about?

DEFINE

Define righteous and righteousness.

RESPOND

In each use of the word "righteous" or "righteousness" in today's Scripture reading, what or who does this word describe?

RESPOND

Why is it important that God is righteous?

Read Jeremiah 23:5–6 again.

Jesus is the "Branch for David." God made a covenant with David that his throne would last forever (2 Samuel 7). Jesus is the righteous offspring who fulfills that promise. One day, we will dwell with Him securely. Draw a tree trunk below. Then, to make the branches, list ways you can be hopeful as you await Christ's return.

DRAW

Read Jeremiah 23:5–6 one more time.

Make a chart below to compare how Jesus is righteous and how, apart from Christ, mankind is not.

Romans 3:22a tells us, "The righteousness of God is through faith in Jesus Christ to all who believe." In light of this truth, write a prayer, thanking Jesus for salvation and the righteousness He imparts to you through faith.

DAY 05: GRACIOUS

The Lord passed in front of him and proclaimed: The Lord—the Lord is a compassionate and gracious God, slow to anger and abounding in faithful love and truth, maintaining faithful love to a thousand generations, forgiving iniquity, rebellion, and sin.

EXODUS 34:6–7A

Read Exodus 34:6–7a.

RESPOND

God is speaking these words about Himself to Moses. Write down each of the adjectives God uses to describe Himself. Then list how He has displayed each of them in your own life for His glory. How do these adjectives show God's graciousness?

MIDDAY

Read Exodus 34:6–7a aloud.

Pray this prayer aloud to God:

> *Lord,*
>
> *Thank You for Your compassion, which grants mercy to my sinful heart.*
>
> *Thank You for Your graciousness to provide Jesus to save me.*
>
> *Thank You for withholding Your anger toward me and granting me salvation.*
>
> *I praise You for Your faithful love and truth that abound in my life.*
>
> *You are faithful to all generations through the gift of Jesus.*
>
> *Thank You for forgiving me of my sin and rebellion and calling me to Yourself.*
>
> *May my mouth be filled with praise and honor to You all day long (Psalm 71:8).*
>
> *Amen.*

PRAY

Read Exodus 34:6–7a one more time.

RESPOND

How have you witnessed God's graciousness in your life?

RESPOND

The psalmist who wrote Psalm 71:8 declares that his mouth praises and honors the Lord all day long. Think about the words you speak. Do you praise and honor God? How does meditating on Scripture help you praise and honor God?

PRAY

Take a few moments to confess the sin and rebellion in your life. Seek forgiveness from the Lord, who is gracious toward you and faithful to forgive.

DAY 06: HOLY

In the year that King Uzziah died, I saw the Lord seated on a high and lofty throne, and the hem of his robe filled the temple. Seraphim were standing above him; they each had six wings: with two they covered their faces, with two they covered their feet, and with two they flew. And one called to another: Holy, holy, holy is the Lord of Armies; his glory fills the whole earth.

ISAIAH 6:1–3

Read Isaiah 6:1–3.

RESPOND

Describe how the glory of the Lord fills the whole earth. Where do you see His glory in nature, humans, etc.?

MEDITATE

Picture yourself in a throne room, and you can only see the hem of God's robe because His glory and holiness are so great. Like Isaiah, you would fall face down before the Lord. Write a prayer of worship and meditate on God's holiness, which is His perfect goodness and righteousness.

Read Isaiah 6:1–3 again.

Draw a picture of the angels, known as Seraphim, based on their description in this passage. Then write "holy" three times. Think about praising the Lord for all eternity, and thank Him that in His holiness, He is divine, pure, and righteous.

DRAW

Read Isaiah 6:1–3 one more time.

RESPOND

In His perfect, holy state, God is sinless and cannot be in the presence of sin. How has He given you the ability to approach His throne with confidence and dwell with Him forever?

RESPOND

Do you know Jesus as your Lord and Savior? If so, praise Him for His sacrifice that gives you the ability to come before our Holy God. If not, search your heart, and ask Jesus to draw you to Him for salvation.

RESPOND

What do you look forward to the most one day when you will be in the presence of our Holy God forever?

DAY 07: COMPASSIONATE

*As a father has compassion on his children,
so the Lord has compassion on those who fear him.*

PSALM 103:13

Read Psalm 103:13.

DEFINE

Define compassion.

RESPOND

How do earthly fathers show compassion to their children?

RESPOND

How does your heavenly Father show you compassion?

RESPOND

Whether your earthly father was good, difficult, or absent, how can you trust your heavenly Father to always have compassion on you?

MIDDAY

Read Psalm 103:13 again. This time, reflect on what it means that "the Lord has compassion on those who fear him." Fill out the chart below. Reflect on what it looks like to trust God over man. How can you trust your Father will show you compassion, even as you fear Him?

	WHAT IT LOOKS LIKE WHEN I FEAR MAN	WHAT IT LOOKS LIKE WHEN I FEAR GOD
RESPOND		

Read Psalm 103:13 one more time.

Write a prayer, thanking God for being the perfect Father. Thank Him for His compassion and His grace in sacrificing His own Son on your behalf. Give Him praise for being powerful, majestic, and worthy of all worship.

PRAY

DAY 08: LOVING

For God loved the world in this way: He gave his one and only Son, so that everyone who believes in him will not perish but have eternal life. For God did not send his Son into the world to condemn the world, but to save the world through him.

JOHN 3:16–17

Read John 3:16–17.

DEFINE

How does the world define love?

DEFINE

Based on these verses, how does God define love?

RESPOND

If God sacrificed His own Son to show His love for you, how should you show love to others?

RESPOND

What do these verses teach you about God and His character?

Write out John 3:16–17 below.

As you write, capitalize "God" and all of His pronouns. Then write this verse: "But God proves his own love for us in that while we were still sinners, Christ died for us" (Romans 5:8). Out of His abundant love, God has given us salvation through Jesus. Spend the afternoon thanking God for this great gift of love.

Read John 3:16–17 again.

PRAY

How would you explain these verses to a friend or family member who does not know the love of Jesus? How can you tangibly show them love so that they see Christ in your life? Reflect on 1 John 4:19, which says, "We love because he first loved us." Then, pray for that friend or family member who needs to know Jesus as their Lord and Savior.

DAY 09: ALL-KNOWING

Oh, the depth of the riches and the wisdom and the knowledge of God! How unsearchable his judgments and untraceable his ways! For who has known the mind of the Lord? Or who has been his counselor? And who has ever given to God, that he should be repaid? For from him and through him and to him are all things. To him be the glory forever. Amen.

ROMANS 11:33–36

Read Romans 11:33–36.

In the Bible, these verses are written as a hymn of praise to the Lord. Write your own hymn or prayer of praise to God based on these verses.

WRITE

MIDDAY

Read Romans 11:33–36 again.

RESPOND

How do these verses show that God is omniscient (all-knowing)?

RESPOND

How do the three questions in the passage give you confidence in God?

RESPOND

What is that one thing in your life you do not trust God with yet?

RESPOND

In what ways can these verses help you hand that thing over to God, knowing that He sees the whole picture of your life, and He has a plan?

Read Romans 11:33–36 one more time.

Rewrite these verses below. When you come to the three questions, write "NO ONE" after each. Take some time to pray and thank the Lord that He is all-knowing and that you can trust Him with every aspect of your life.

WRITE

DAY 10: ETERNAL

Trust in the Lord forever, because in the Lord,
the Lord himself, is an everlasting rock!

ISAIAH 26:4

Read Isaiah 26:4.

RESPOND

How many times is the name "Lord" mentioned in this verse?

RESPOND

What does it mean to be "an everlasting rock"?

RESPOND

Do you believe that God is a firm foundation? In what storm of life can you praise Him for being your rock?

RESPOND

"Everlasting" also means "eternal." What does it mean that God is eternal? Why is that important?

MIDDAY

Read Isaiah 26:4 again.

Make a chart with two columns. On one side, write down the events in life in which you trusted God as your rock. In the other column, write those circumstances in which you still struggle to see God as your everlasting rock. Take some time to pray over those things, and give them to the Lord.

PRAY

Write Isaiah 26:4 three times below. Try to memorize it as you write. This verse will provide encouragement through the storms of life as you remember God is your rock for eternity.

WRITE

DAY 11: SHEPHERD

He himself bore our sins in his body on the tree; so that, having died to sins, we might live for righteousness. By his wounds you have been healed. For you were like sheep going astray, but you have now returned to the Shepherd and Overseer of your souls.

1 PETER 2:24–25

Read 1 Peter 2:24–25.

Draw some sheep below. Inside each one, write what makes you go astray from the Lord. What causes you to wander from your faith and the safe care of the Shepherd?

DRAW

MIDDAY

Read 1 Peter 2:24–25 again.

DEFINE

What is a "Shepherd and Overseer"?

RESPOND

How did Jesus bring His sinful sheep back into the fold?

RESPOND

What does it mean for you to die to sin?

RESPOND

How did Jesus's wounds heal you?

RESPOND

Think back to your picture of sheep on the previous page. What do you need to confess to your Shepherd? What sinful part of your life needs to die?

RESPOND

In what ways can Jesus shepherd your heart? How can you live for righteousness?

Read 1 Peter 2:24–25 one more time.

Jesus gave His very life to save His sheep. Write a prayer of thanksgiving for the sacrifice He made on your behalf. Praise Him that you are not left to the wolves of this world. He has your heart in His hand and will guide you in His righteous way.

PRAY

DAY 12: MERCIFUL

But God, who is rich in mercy, because of his great love that he had for us, made us alive with Christ even though we were dead in trespasses. You are saved by grace!

EPHESIANS 2:4–5

*Read Ephesians 2:4–5. Then read each verse entry below, and focus on the words in **bold** each time. Journal your thoughts and observations in response to the **bolded** words. What do they teach you about God and His character?*

But God, who is rich in mercy, because of his great love that he had for us,

But God, who is **rich in mercy**, because of his great love that he had for us,

But God, who is rich in mercy, because of **his great love** that he had for us,

made us alive with Christ even though we were dead in trespasses. You are saved by grace!

made us alive with Christ even though we were dead in trespasses. **You are saved by grace!**

Read Ephesians 2:4–5 again.

Rewrite these verses in your own words. How would you explain them to a friend or family member who does not know Jesus?

WRITE

Read Ephesians 2:4–5 one more time.

How has God shown His mercy and love toward you? Write your testimony below. Reminding yourself of God's mercy and saving grace will help you remember what Jesus has done for you.

WRITE

DAY 13: FAITHFUL

Let the whole earth shout triumphantly to the Lord! Serve the Lord with gladness; come before him with joyful songs. Acknowledge that the Lord is God. He made us, and we are his—his people, the sheep of his pasture. Enter his gates with thanksgiving and his courts with praise. Give thanks to him and bless his name. For the Lord is good, and his faithful love endures forever; his faithfulness, through all generations.

PSALM 100:1–5

Read Psalm 100:1–5.

The psalmist gives us six commands in this passage. Using the prompts, list them out below.

1. SHOUT

2. SERVE

3. COME

4. ACKNOWLEDGE

5. ENTER

6. GIVE THANKS

JOURNAL

MIDDAY

Read Psalm 100:1–5 again.

WRITE

Rewrite the last verse three times.

RESPOND

How does this verse teach you to rely on God in your current season of life?

RESPOND

How has God shown His faithfulness to you in your current season?

RESPOND

What is something good the Father has given to you today?

Read Psalm 100:1–5 one more time. Do the exercises below.

RESPOND

1. Shout for joy over something the Lord has given you triumph over.

2. Consider how you can intentionally serve Him with gladness tomorrow.

3. Sing a hymn or praise song to Him as you make dinner or get ready for bed.

4. Acknowledge God's sovereignty in your life, and thank Him that you are one of His sheep.

5. Enter God's presence through prayer. Praise Him for His goodness and faithfulness to all generations.

6. Give thanks for all aspects of your day, good or bad. God is faithful and in control.

DAY 14: RIGHTEOUS

For I am not ashamed of the gospel, because it is the power of God for salvation to everyone who believes, first to the Jew, and also to the Greek. For in it the righteousness of God is revealed from faith to faith, just as it is written: The righteous will live by faith.

ROMANS 1:16–17

Read Romans 1:16–17.

RESPOND

What does it mean to "not be ashamed of the gospel"?

RESPOND

Why is it important that both Jews and Greeks are given salvation?

RESPOND

How are you made righteous?

Read Romans 1:16–17 again.

Draw a picture of the cross on a hill. At the base of the cross, write down all those sins you are unsure how to leave behind. Take some time to kneel before the Lord in prayer, and leave these things at the cross. Jesus washed away your sin and made you righteous before the Father!

DRAW

Read Romans 1:16–17 one more time.

PRAY

With whom are you scared to share the gospel? Ask God to give you the boldness to not be ashamed of the gospel.

PRAY

In what area of your life do you struggle to walk by faith? Ask God to help you live your life for Him, clothed in His righteousness because of Christ.

PRAY

End your day in praise to God. Praise Him for salvation, faith, and righteousness!

DAY 15: HOLY

The Lord spoke to Moses: "Speak to the entire Israelite community and tell them: Be holy because I, the Lord your God, am holy. Each of you is to respect his mother and father. You are to keep my Sabbaths; I am the Lord your God. Do not turn to worthless idols or make cast images of gods for yourselves; I am the Lord your God."

LEVITICUS 19:1–4

Read Leviticus 19:1–4.

Using the acrostic below, utilize each letter to describe an aspect of the holiness of God. For example, H could represent "**H**is perfect nature."

JOURNAL

H

O

L

Y

MIDDAY

Read Leviticus 19:1–4 again.

RESPOND What does it mean that God is holy?

RESPOND List the three ways God mentioned we can display holiness.

RESPOND How can you respect your parents in your current stage of life?

RESPOND Do you honor the Sabbath? How do you incorporate rest into your life?

RESPOND What is something in your life that you make more important than God? How can you destroy this idol?

Read Leviticus 19:1–4 one more time.

In the space below, rewrite the passage in your own words. Use it as a prayer to pray back to God, thanking Him for His holiness and asking Him to help you be holy.

WRITE

DAY 16: GOOD

Do not remember the sins of my youth or my acts of rebellion; in keeping with your faithful love, remember me because of your goodness, Lord. The Lord is good and upright; therefore he shows sinners the way. He leads the humble in what is right and teaches them his way.

PSALM 25:7–9

Read Psalm 25:7–9.

In His goodness, the Lord shows His children the right way to live. Draw two roads below. On the first road, write the sins and distractions that keep you from God when you go your own way. On the second road, write what truths keep you on the path toward God and His goodness.

DRAW

Read Psalm 25:7–9 again.

Some of the words used to define "good" are listed below. Based on these verses in Psalms, how do these words help us better understand God's goodness?

VIRTUOUS:

RIGHT:

RESPOND

KIND:

RELIABLE:

Read Psalm 25:7–9 one more time.

RESPOND

How has God revealed His goodness in your life today?

RESPOND

What sinful habits and acts of rebellion do you need to lay aside?

RESPOND

How have you seen God teach you His way?

RESPOND

Why is Jesus the ultimate good in your life?

PRAY

Write a prayer, thanking God for His goodness to lead you on His upright path. Ask for humility to repent of your sinful and rebellious ways. Thank God for His faithful love.

DAY 17: UNCHANGING

In the beginning, Lord, you established the earth, and the heavens are the works of your hands; they will perish, but you remain. They will all wear out like clothing; you will roll them up like a cloak, and they will be changed like clothing. But you are the same, and your years will never end.

HEBREWS 1:10 – 12

*Read Hebrews 1:10–12. Then read each verse entry below, and focus on the words in **bold** each time. Journal your thoughts and observations in response to the **bolded** words. What do they teach you about our unchanging God?*

JOURNAL

In the beginning, Lord, you established the earth,

In the beginning, Lord, **you established the earth**,

and the heavens are the works of your hands; **they will perish**, but you remain.

and the heavens are the works of your hands; they will perish, **but you remain**.

They will all wear out like clothing; you will roll them up like a cloak, and they will be changed like clothing.

But **you are the same**, and **your years will never end**.

MIDDAY

Read Hebrews 1:10–12 again.

RESPOND

What aspects of your life seem to be unsteady or changing currently?

RESPOND

How do these verses about God's unchanging nature encourage you in those areas?

RESPOND

In what ways did Jesus prove His unchanging nature on the cross? Why can you trust Him?

Read Hebrews 1:10–12 one more time.

PRAY

Spend some time in prayer. First, if you are able, bow on your knees. Then, hold out your hands with palms up. Picture all your fleeting, changing, perishing concerns in your hands, and offer them to God in prayer. Seek forgiveness where needed and encouragement to press on. Allow our unchanging God to take hold of your life, and thank Him that He is always the same.

DAY 18: HEALER

He himself bore our sins in his body on the tree; so that, having died to sins, we might live for righteousness. By his wounds you have been healed.

I PETER 2:24

Read 1 Peter 2:24.

RESPOND

Who is this Scripture passage about?

RESPOND

How does Jesus bring healing to your sinful heart?

RESPOND

Once Jesus heals our sinful hearts, how do we live for Him?

RESPOND

In what ways can you die to sin daily? What sin do you need to die to today?

Read 1 Peter 2:24 again.

Rewrite the verse three times in the space below. Each time you write it, try to commit it to memory. On days you struggle with your sin, speak this verse, knowing Jesus has conquered sin on your behalf and can provide victory.

WRITE

Read 1 Peter 2:24 one more time.

The verse says, "By His wounds you have been healed." List some of your sins below, and then, next to each of them, write examples of how Jesus heals you and gives you victory over them. Then, take some time to pray and thank Him for the sacrifice of His life that gives you healing from all sin and the ability to have an abundant life in Christ.

PRAY

DAY 19: PEACE

Don't worry about anything, but in everything, through prayer and petition with thanksgiving, present your requests to God. And the peace of God, which surpasses all understanding, will guard your hearts and minds in Christ Jesus.

PHILIPPIANS 4:6−7

Read Philippians 4:6–7.

RESPOND

Why does God tell us not to worry about anything?

RESPOND

How do these verses define the "peace of God"?

RESPOND

What role does Jesus play in bringing peace to your heart?

PRAY

What is the thing you have worried about most lately? As you go through the morning, practice giving it to God over and over again in prayer.

Read Philippians 4:6–7 again.

Draw a large heart below. Take a few moments to record all your worries and concerns inside the heart. Now, with your pen, draw a cross over the top of the heart. Spend some time in prayer, giving your heart and all its worries and concerns to Jesus. The work He did on the cross to bring salvation gave us new hearts. He will guard your heart and mind and bring you peace.

Read Philippians 4:6–7 one more time.

PRAY

This verse reminds us to present all our requests to God. This includes the requests you think are impossible for even God to answer. He is capable of shouldering all your cares and replacing them with His peace in your life. Take some time to pray again. Continue giving the cares, worries, or anxieties that are nagging you over to God.

DAY 20: TRUTH

He has shown his people the power of his works by giving them the inheritance of the nations. The works of his hands are truth and justice; all his instructions are trustworthy. They are established forever and ever, enacted in truth and in uprightness.

PSALM 111:6–8

Read Psalm 111:6–8.

RESPOND

How do these verses describe the works of God's hands?
List all six descriptions below. (Hint: one is listed twice.)

1.

2.

3.

4.

5.

6.

REFLECT

Reflect on the six descriptions of the work of God's
hands that you listed above. What does each one of
these attributes teach you about God's character?

Read Psalm 111:6–8 again.

Draw a picture of some hands below. Imagine them to be God's hands. These verses remind us that He is true, trustworthy, and upright. Take a moment, and think about the lies you believe about yourself and this world, and then record those lies on the hands. Spend some time in prayer, asking God to show you His truth and turning over to His capable hands all the lies you are tempted to believe.

DRAW

Read Psalm 111:6–8 one more time.

DEFINE

What is the world's definition of truth?

DEFINE

How does God define truth?

RESPOND

What lies does Satan attempt to tell you about God and His ways? How can you fight back?

RESPOND

How can the Bible instruct you in the true and trustworthy ways of God?

DAY 21: PATIENT

Dear friends, don't overlook this one fact: With the Lord one day is like a thousand years, and a thousand years like one day. The Lord does not delay his promise, as some understand delay, but is patient with you, not wanting any to perish but all to come to repentance.

2 PETER 3:8 – 9

Read 2 Peter 3:8–9.

RESPOND

How has God shown His patience to the world?

RESPOND

How has God shown His patience toward you?

RESPOND

In what ways do you need to exhibit patience in your life as you await Christ's return?

RESPOND

Why is it a blessing that the Lord patiently delays Christ's return? How can you serve Him until He returns?

MIDDAY

Read 2 Peter 3:8–9 again.

Draw a timeline below. Think of a season or event in your life when you felt like God was not working, but as you look back, you can clearly see He was at work. Record on your timeline the ways God patiently and sovereignly directed your steps during that season. Then spend some time in prayer, thanking Him for His patience as He works to bring the world to repentance and uses you as part of His perfect plan.

DRAW

Read 2 Peter 3:8–9 one more time.

Merriam-Webster defines "patience" as "able to remain calm and not become annoyed when waiting for a long time or when dealing with problems or difficult people; done in a careful way over a long period of time without hurrying." List below how God exhibits this definition perfectly. Then take some time to pray, asking the Lord to help you exhibit patience so that others will be drawn toward Christ.

PRAY

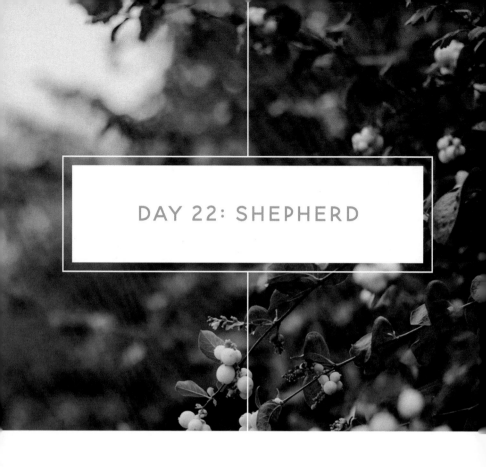

DAY 22: SHEPHERD

The Lord is my shepherd; I have what I need. He lets me lie down in green pastures; He leads me beside quiet waters. He renews my life; he leads me along the right paths for his name's sake.

PSALM 23:1–3

*Read Psalm 23:1–3. Read each verse entry below, and focus on the words in **bold** each time. Journal your thoughts and observations in response to the **bolded** words. What do they teach you about God and His character?*

JOURNAL

The Lord is my shepherd; I have what I need.

The Lord is my shepherd; **I have what I need**.

He lets me lie down in green pastures; He leads me beside quiet waters.

He lets me lie down in green pastures; **He leads me** beside quiet waters.

He renews my life; he leads me along the right paths for his name's sake.

He renews my life; **he leads me along the right paths** for his name's sake.

He renews my life; he leads me along the right paths **for his name's sake**.

Read Psalm 23:1–3 again.

Using the acrostic below, utilize each letter to describe the Lord as our shepherd. For example, S could represent "**s**afe" or "**s**overeign."

S

H

E

P

H

E

R

D

RESPOND

Read Psalm 23:1–3 one more time.

Spend some time in prayer before the evening draws to a close. Use the prompts below to guide your prayer time.

1. Thank the Lord that He is your Good Shepherd.

2. Thank Him for giving you all you need.

3. Praise Him for rest and renewal in your life.

4. Ask Him to continue to lead you on the right path and keep you from sin.

5. Praise Him for working in your life in order to bring Him glory.

RESPOND

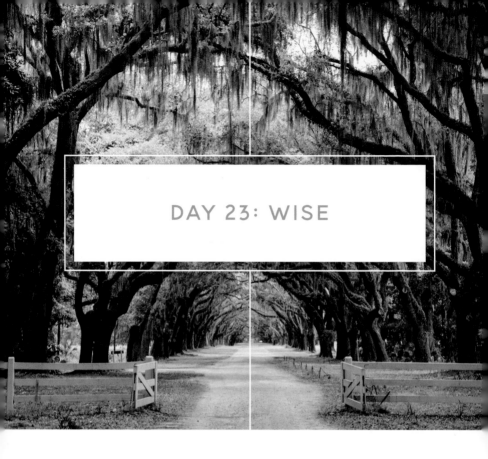

DAY 23: WISE

Yet to those who are called, both Jews and Greeks, Christ is the power of God and the wisdom of God, because God's foolishness is wiser than human wisdom, and God's weakness is stronger than human strength.

I CORINTHIANS 1:24–25

Read 1 Corinthians 1:24–25.

DEFINE

How does the world define wisdom?

RESPOND

According to this verse, who embodies wisdom?

RESPOND

Why is it important that this message is addressed to both Jews and Greeks?

RESPOND

How did Christ's "weakness" on the cross show His ultimate power?

RESPOND

How do these verses encourage you in your own weakness?

RESPOND

Do you value the weakness in your life? How can it remind you to rely on God's wisdom?

MIDDAY

Read 1 Corinthians 1:24–25 again.

Draw a chart below with two columns. On the left side, record areas in your life where you have felt weak or foolish. On the right side, record how God, through His wisdom and power, used those situations to teach you, encourage you, and bring Him glory.

DRAW

Read 1 Corinthians 1:24–25 one more time.

Think back over your day. How did God reveal His wisdom in your life today? How do you see Him working to grow you in maturity and wisdom? Spend some time in prayer. Ask God to help you grow in your walk with Him. Ask Him to give you wisdom to discern the right decisions and relationships for you. Record your thoughts below.

PRAY

DAY 24: SOVEREIGN

This is what the Lord, the King of Israel and its Redeemer, the Lord of Armies, says: I am the first and I am the last. There is no God but me. Who, like me, can announce the future? Let him say so and make a case before me, since I have established an ancient people. Let these gods declare the coming things, and what will take place. Do not be startled or afraid. Have I not told you and declared it long ago? You are my witnesses! Is there any God but me? There is no other Rock; I do not know any.

ISAIAH 44:6–8

Read Isaiah 44:6–8.

In the space below, list all the names of God you find in these verses. Next to each one, describe how this name displays His sovereignty.

Read Isaiah 44:6–8 again.

RESPOND

What false gods does the world try to place above God?

RESPOND

In what ways does it comfort you to read of God's sovereignty over all things in these verses?

RESPOND

According to these verses, why can we "not be startled or afraid"?

RESPOND

How does Jesus make you a part of God's ancient people?

RESPOND

How can you be a witness to God's sovereignty to others?

Read Isaiah 44:6–8 one more time.

In what area of your life are you currently struggling to see God's sovereignty? Use the space below to record your concerns, and then write out a prayer thanking God that He is Lord, King of Israel, Redeemer, Lord of Armies, first and last, God, and Rock. Ask Him to show you how He has been sovereign in your current season of life.

PRAY

DAY 25: LOVING

Whoever confesses that Jesus is the Son of God—God remains in him and he in God. And we have come to know and to believe the love that God has for us. God is love, and the one who remains in love remains in God, and God remains in him.

1 JOHN 4:15–16

Read 1 John 4:15–16.

WRITE

Write out these verses below. Then, draw a heart around the word "love" each time it is listed. Next, draw a box around the word "remain." Lastly, circle each time you see "God."

MEDITATE

How do these three words define the relationship God has with us? Spend the morning meditating on God's love for you through the gift of Jesus.

MIDDAY

Read 1 John 4:15–16 again.

DRAW

In the space below, draw a large heart. Inside the heart, write a sentence that declares your love and devotion to Jesus.

RESPOND

How does your declaration for Christ allow you to remain in God and He in you?

RESPOND

In what ways have you "come to know and to believe the love that God has for" you?

Read 1 John 4:15–16 one more time.

RESPOND

Merriam-Webster's dictionary defines "remain" as "to continue unchanged." How does God's love continue unchanged in your life?

RESPOND

How does having God's love remain in you help you love others, even when they are hard to love?

RESPOND

Who in your life needs to hear your testimony of God's love? How can you encourage them to confess Christ and remain in His love?

PRAY

Spend some time in prayer, asking God to direct you to the people who most need to experience His love through you.

DAY 26: UNCHANGING

Every good and perfect gift is from above, coming down from the Father of lights, who does not change like shifting shadows.

JAMES 1:17

Read James 1:17.

JOURNAL

Take some time to list the good and perfect gifts from God in your life. How does each one show His unchanging love for you?

*Read James 1:17 again. Read each verse entry below, and focus on the words in **bold** each time. Journal your thoughts and observations in response to the **bolded** words. What do they teach you about God and His unchanging character?*

Every good and perfect gift is from above,

Every good and perfect gift is **from above,**

coming down from the Father of lights, who does not change like shifting shadows.

coming down from the Father of lights, **who does not change like shifting shadows**.

JOURNAL

Read James 1:17 one more time.

PRAY

We often think "good and perfect gifts" are those things that bring us happiness or ease in our lives. Think of a season or event in your life that was hard. How might that have been a "good and perfect gift" from God that drew you closer to Him? Spend some time in prayer. Thank God for all His gifts that are just what we need, even if we do not see them as good. Ask the Lord to help you view His unchanging character as one of His many good gifts.

DAY 27: JUST

For I will proclaim the Lord's name. Declare the greatness of our God!
The Rock—his work is perfect; all his ways are just. A faithful God,
without bias, he is righteous and true.

DEUTERONOMY 32:3–4

Read Deuteronomy 32:3–4.

RESPOND

How do these verses describe God's just ways?

RESPOND

Do you believe all of God's ways are just? In what areas do you struggle with God's justice: in your own life, in others' lives, or both?

RESPOND

Why can you trust God's ways are just?

RESPOND

How can you proclaim God's just character to others and declare His greatness?

RESPOND

How does Jesus allow us to stand before our just God?

MIDDAY

Read Deuteronomy 32:3–4 again.

Draw a large rectangle below. Then pretend you are designing a billboard. Write a message inside the billboard that declares God's greatness. Think about this message as you go through your afternoon. Does your life proclaim this message to others? If not, how can you grow in this?

DRAW

Read Deuteronomy 32:3–4 one more time.

These verses are part of 43 others known as the "Song of Moses." They are the words Moses shared with the people of Israel before his death, reminding them that God is both just and gracious. The people were called to obey God and remember His faithfulness and love. If you were to write a final message to your family and friends about God's justice and faithfulness, what would you share? Record your thoughts below.

WRITE

DAY 28: TRUTH

The Word became flesh and dwelt among us. We observed his glory, the glory as the one and only Son from the Father, full of grace and truth.

JOHN 1:14

Read John 1:14.

Use the space below to write out this verse three times.
Use it as an exercise to memorize this important passage.

WRITE

MIDDAY

Read John 1:14 again.

RESPOND   Who is the Word that became flesh?

RESPOND   How does Jesus reveal God's glory?

RESPOND   How does Jesus becoming flesh reflect God's grace and truth?

RESPOND   In what ways does this verse display Jesus as fully God and fully man?

RESPOND   How has God shown you grace?

RESPOND   Why is it important that God is truth?

Read John 1:14 one more time.

God is truth! It is against His very nature to lie. Draw a chart with two columns below. On the left side, record the lies the world tells us to believe (some examples may include: religion is a crutch, you can do anything if you try hard enough, your worth is found in money, etc.). On the right side, record God's truth against those lies. Then, take some time to pray against those lies, and recite Psalm 25:5 back to the Lord: "Guide me in your truth and teach me, for you are the God of my salvation; I wait for you all day long."

DRAW

DAY 29: REFUGE

I love you, Lord, my strength. The Lord is my rock, my fortress, and my deliverer, my God, my rock where I seek refuge, my shield and the horn of my salvation, my stronghold. I called to the Lord, who is worthy of praise, and I was saved from my enemies.

PSALM 18:1–3

Read Psalm 18:1–3.

RESPOND

Using the acrostic below, utilize each letter to describe the Lord as our refuge. For example, R could represent "**r**ock," or F could represent "**f**ortress."

R

E

F

U

G

E

MIDDAY

Read Psalm 18:1–3 again.

Use the space below to draw a wall of bricks. Inside each brick, list the experiences and seasons when God has protected or saved you and the people He used in your life during those times. How has He been a fortress, refuge, and source of salvation for you in these things? Spend some time in prayer, thanking God for His salvation and great love. Praise Him for being your deliverer and shield.

DRAW

Read Psalm 18:1–3 one more time.

Take some time to think about the words listed below.
How does each one illustrate God's character?
Journal your thoughts, and say a brief prayer
of praise after each entry.

ROCK

STRONGHOLD

REFUGE

FORTRESS

STRENGTH

DELIVERER

SHIELD

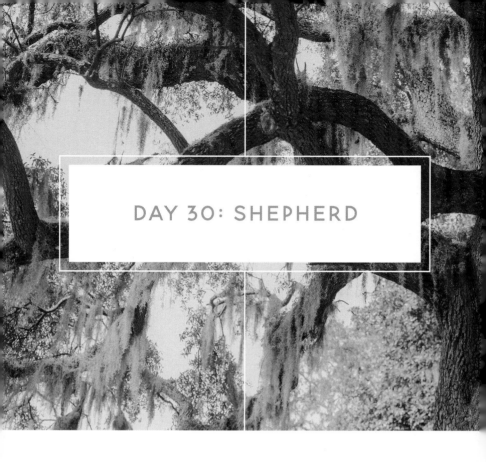

DAY 30: SHEPHERD

For the Lamb who is at the center of the throne will shepherd them; he will guide them to springs of the waters of life, and God will wipe away every tear from their eyes.

REVELATION 7:17

*Read Revelation 7:17. Read each verse entry below, and focus on the words in **bold** each time. Journal your thoughts and observations in response to the **bolded** words. What do they teach you about God as our eternal Shepherd?*

For **the Lamb** who is at the center of the throne
will shepherd them;

For the Lamb who is **at the center of the throne**
will shepherd them;

For the Lamb who is at the center of the throne
will shepherd them;

he will guide them to springs of the waters of life,

he will guide them **to springs of the waters of life,**

and **God will wipe away every tear** from their eyes.

JOURNAL

Read Revelation 7:17 again.

One day, Jesus will return for His children and shepherd us home to our eternal dwelling place with God. All sin and sorrow will be gone. There will be no more tears. What are some things in our world you are looking forward to leaving behind? What do you look forward to most about heaven one day?

RESPOND

Read Revelation 7:17 one more time.

In the book of Revelation, over and over again, the elders and angels bow before the throne in worship. As you end your day, and if you are physically able, kneel to the Lord in worship and prayer. Spend some time worshiping our Great Shepherd in prayer or song or quoting Scripture. Then, pray for those who do not yet know Christ. Pray they will draw near to our Shepherd before it is too late.

PRAY

DAY 31: FAITHFUL

Give thanks to the Lord, for he is good; his faithful love endures forever.

PSALM 107:1

Read Psalm 107:1.

RESPOND — According to the second half of Psalm 107:1, why is the Lord good?

RESPOND — How is the Lord faithful to His promises?

RESPOND — In what ways have you seen the love of God endure through history?

RESPOND — What are some ways you can live your life as a testimony to God's goodness and faithfulness?

RESPOND — How have you seen God's faithfulness in your life this past week, month, and year?

Read Psalm 107:1 aloud.

Write the verse five times below. Use this as a time to commit this verse to memory. In seasons of joy and hardship, quote this verse to remind yourself of God's faithfulness in everything.

WRITE

Read or recite Psalm 107:1 one more time.

PRAY

As you end this month-long journey of meditating on God's character, what trait has stood out to you the most? Which one would you like to study and understand more? How can you continue to grow in your knowledge and understanding of God's character? Record your answers below. Then, spend some time in prayer, thanking God for this journey and all He has taught you. Ask Him to continue to grow you and make you more and more like Jesus as you await His return.

Thank you for studying
God's Word with us!

CONNECT WITH US

@thedailygraceco
@dailygracepodcast

CONTACT US

info@thedailygraceco.com

SHARE

#thedailygraceco

VISIT US ONLINE

www.thedailygraceco.com

MORE DAILY GRACE

The Daily Grace App
Daily Grace Podcast